IT'S TIME TO EAT FIGS

It's Time to Eat FIGS

Walter the Educator

Silent King Books
A WhichHead Entertainment Imprint

Copyright © 2024 by Walter the Educator

All rights reserved. No part of this book may be reproduced in any manner whatsoever without written per- mission except in the case of brief quotations embodied in critical articles and reviews.

First Printing, 2024

Disclaimer

This book is a literary work; the story is not about specific persons, locations, situations, and/or circumstances unless mentioned in a historical context. Any resemblance to real persons, locations, situations, and/or circumstances is coincidental. This book is for entertainment and informational purposes only. The author and publisher offer this information without warranties expressed or implied. No matter the grounds, neither the author nor the publisher will be accountable for any losses, injuries, or other damages caused by the reader's use of this book. The use of this book acknowledges an understanding and acceptance of this disclaimer.

It's Time to Eat FIGS is a collectible early learning book by Walter the Educator suitable for all ages belonging to Walter the Educator's Time to Eat Book Series. Collect more books at WaltertheEducator.com

USE THE EXTRA SPACE TO TAKE NOTES AND DOCUMENT YOUR MEMORIES

FIGS

It's fig time now, come gather near,

It's Time to Eat

Figs

A tasty fruit we hold so dear!

Soft and round with a purple hue,

Figs are sweet and good for you.

Pick one up and take a peek,

Outside smooth, inside unique!

With tiny seeds and syrupy flow,

Figs are a treat that make you glow.

Eat them fresh or dried and sweet,

Figs are such a yummy treat!

Soft and chewy, they're so fun,

A little snack for everyone!

Figs grow high on a leafy tree,

Nature's gift for you and me.

Plucked by hand with gentle care,

They're a treasure beyond compare.

It's Time to Eat

Figs

Packed with goodness, fiber, too,

Figs help keep you strong and true.

With every bite, your body will cheer,

Figs are healthy all through the year!

In pies or jam, or on some bread,

Figs make a feast that's widely spread.

Their syrupy taste is rich and fine,

A flavor that feels just divine.

Soft and wrinkly or smooth and new,

Figs come in shades of purple and blue.

A golden fig is rare and bright,

A little gem, a pure delight!

One for breakfast, one for a snack,

Figs are the fruit you'll always pack.

Sweet like honey, soft as a cloud,

It's Time to Eat

Figs

Eating figs will make you proud!

Let's share some figs with family and friends,

A treat that brings joy that never ends.

It's fig time now, so take a bite,

This fruity snack feels just right!

So pick a fig and start the fun,

A special fruit for everyone.

Figs are ready, don't wait too late,

It's Time to Eat

Figs

It's fig time now, so grab a plate!

ABOUT THE CREATOR

Walter the Educator is one of the pseudonyms for Walter Anderson. Formally educated in Chemistry, Business, and Education, he is an educator, an author, a diverse entrepreneur, and he is the son of a disabled war veteran. "Walter the Educator" shares his time between educating and creating. He holds interests and owns several creative projects that entertain, enlighten, enhance, and educate, hoping to inspire and motivate you. Follow, find new works, and stay up to date with Walter the Educator™

at WaltertheEducator.com

www.ingramcontent.com/pod-product-compliance
Lightning Source LLC
LaVergne TN
LVHW052012060526
838201LV00059B/3984